GCSE
English
PUNCTUATION & GRAMMAR

Catherine Hilton
Margaret Hyder

Letts

EDUCATIONAL

Every effort has been made to trace copyright holders and to obtain their permission for the use of copyright material. The author and publishers will gladly receive information enabling them to rectify any error or omission in subsequent editions.

First published 1997
Reprinted 1998

Letts Educational
Schools and Colleges Division
9–15 Aldine Street
London W12 8AW
Telephone: 0181 740 2270

Text: ©MCH 1997
Design and illustrations ©BPP (Letts Educational) Ltd 1997

Design, page layout and illustrations by Moondisks Ltd, Cambridge

British Library Cataloguing-in-Publication Data
A CIP record for this book is available from the British Library

ISBN 1 84085 1406

Printed and bound in Great Britain

Letts Educational is the trading name of BPP (Letts Educational) Ltd

Contents

Introduction

This book is divided into two sections:

    punctuation

    grammar.

Although you can work through each section independently, you may find that you need to refer to points in the *Grammar* section when you are reading the *Punctuation* section and vice versa. We refer you to the appropriate chapter in the other section where we feel this may be helpful, but you can always refer to another chapter or the glossary if you want to clarify any points.

Punctuation

Each chapter deals with a specific punctuation mark. You are shown the main rules governing the use of punctuation marks and given advice about how to use them in your writing. You may work through the chapters in any order, but if you feel you need quite a bit of help with punctuation then you might find it easier to read through the chapters in the order they appear in this section.

Grammar

Each chapter deals with a particular part of speech:

nouns

pronouns

verbs

adjectives

adverbs

prepositions

You may decide to work through the chapters systematically or dip into chapters in any order you wish. It is unlikely you will remember all the information and technical terms we use in this section: the important thing is to understand the functions of words in sentences and avoid common errors. You can always use this section for reference to check any points you are uncertain about.

In some chapters, under the heading **For you to do**, there is an activity for you to undertake.

SECTION 1
punctuation

1 Introducing Punctuation

punctuation, the act or art of dividing sentences by points or marks.

–from *Chambers Concise Dictionary*

What is punctuation

- It is a standard code that everyone can understand.
- It consists of:

full stops

question marks

exclamation marks

commas

apostrophes

quotation marks

semicolons

colons

capital letters

Why is punctuation important?

- It helps you understand what you read.
- It gives your reader clues and information.
- It helps others understand your writing.
- You are awarded marks for punctuation in the GCSE English exam –
  a percentage of marks is awarded for spelling, punctuation and grammar.
- You are awarded marks for punctuation in other GCSE subjects too.

It is worth thinking carefully about punctuation. Remember, every mark in exams is important. It could mean a higher grade.

Common mistakes

Examiners frequently comment that candidates:

- don't write in sentences
- use commas instead of full stops
- use too few commas, or too many commas
- don't use apostrophes
- use apostrophes when they aren't needed.

Checkpoints

- Learn the main uses of each punctuation mark.
- Practise using them.
- Use this book as a reference.
- Ask your teacher if you don't understand how to use a punctuation mark.
- Always check through your work. Have you used punctuation so that others understand exactly what you mean?
- When you are reading, look at how other writers punctuate their work.

You *can* improve your punctuation. It just takes a little time and practice.

2 Sentences

What is a sentence?
- It is a group of words that makes complete sense.
- A sentence has a subject (or *implied* subject – page 6).
- A sentence has at least one verb.
- A sentence can be a *statement, question, command* or *exclamation*.

Why are sentences important?
- They allow listeners and readers to make sense of what you say and write.
- Sentences are a convention – part of standard English.
- They are required in all formal writing situations such as essays, letters, reports and instructions.
- You will lose marks in English exams, and some other exams in which you have to write essays, if you don't write in sentences.

What are the different types of sentence?
Sentences can be
- statements
- questions
- commands
- exclamations.

Statements
- These express a fact or opinion:

  Paul's briefcase burst open. *(fact)*
  I think it is too heavy. *(opinion)*

Questions
- These are sentences which require an answer:

Is it my turn?
Are you going out tonight?

Commands
▨ These give an instruction saying what must or must not be done:
Use two eggs. *(an instruction in a recipe)*
Do *not* run. *(a notice at a swimming pool)*

Exclamations
▨ These show emotional outbursts expressing joy, sorrow, dismay or anger:
What a wonderful day it is!
How dreadful it must have been!

Sentence punctuation
▨ A sentence ends with either a full stop, a question mark or an exclamation mark.
▨ A capital letter is used for the first letter of the first word to indicate clearly the beginning of a sentence.

Sentences make sense
1   hoped to see you
2   Robert plays hockey and football.
3   Clare and John
4   asked me to attend

Only number 2 is a sentence. The rest don't make sense – something is missing.
▨ A sentence is made up of two parts:
▸ the *subject*
▸ the *predicate*.

Subject
▨ The *subject* of a sentence is who or what the sentence is about. For example, in 2 above,
Robert plays hockey and football,
Robert is the subject, as the sentence is about him and what he does.
▨ The subject of a sentence is usually a *noun* or *pronoun*. (See Chapter 15 *Nouns* and Chapter 16 *Pronouns*.)

▦ Every sentence must have a subject.

Examples: **The car** is worth £18,000.
Mrs Gupta lives next door to my aunt.
The door had been painted with fresh red paint.

Implied subject
Don't interfere!
Stop what you are doing please!
Do not smoke in this area.

There doesn't appear to be a subject in each of the sentences above.

▦ In a sentence which gives a command, the subject may not appear, but it is implicit in the meaning of the sentence.

▦ The subject is the person who is being spoken to or who is reading the instruction.

Predicate

▦ The *predicate* provides information about the subject. In the sentence
Robert plays hockey and football,

plays hockey and football is the predicate. It tells us what **Robert** (the subject) does.

▦ The predicate contains a verb: **plays**. A *verb* is an action or a state of being. (There is more about verbs in Chapter 17 *Verbs*.)

▦ A predicate always has a verb in it which gives you information about the subject of the sentence.

Examples: Clare and John **were** in the Golden Cross on Saturday.

subject   predicate

My mother **hoped** to see you.

subject   predicate

Finding the verb

▦ A verb describes an action or a state of being.

Examples: thinks   is   buy
examined   kick

Some verbs are easier to identify than others. When a clear action is taking place, the verb is more obvious.

Examples: The supporters **cheered** their team.
He **whistled** happily.

Sometimes the action is more passive and so more difficult to spot.

Examples: They **have** two kittens. *(The 'action' is 'owning' the kittens.)*

I **am** hungry. **(am** *comes from the verb* **to be** *and here the 'action' is the state of being.)*

If you still aren't certain about the less obvious verbs, turn to page 67 in Chapter 17 *Verbs*.

Finding the subject

Once you have identified the verb in a sentence, look to see who or what is carrying out the action.

Examples: **He** fell down the hole. *(Here the verb is **fell** and **he** is doing the falling, so **he** is the subject.)*

Silver and gold are both precious metals. **(Silver and gold** *are the subject and **are** is the verb.)*

Checkpoints

▓ A sentence can be any length but it must:
   ▷ make sense
   ▷ have a subject (or an implied subject)
   ▷ have at least one verb.
▓ Sentences can be:
   ▷ statements
   ▷ questions
   ▷ commands
   ▷ exclamations.
▓ A sentence must end with a full stop, question mark or exclamation mark.
▓ Every sentence must begin with a capital letter.
▓ Essays, letters, reports and other formal writing tasks should always be written in sentences.
▓ Always check any piece of work to make sure you have written in sentences.
▓ You will find more about different types of sentence in Chapter 3 *More Sentences*.

---

3 More Sentences

In Chapter 2 you were shown that a sentence:
- makes complete sense
- has a verb and a subject
- can be a statement, question, command or exclamation.

This chapter gives you more practice in identifying sentences and looks at four different types of sentence construction: *simple*, *double*, *multiple* and *complex* sentences.

Why is it important to vary sentence structure?
- Being able to use a variety of sentence structures makes your writing and speaking more interesting.
- It allows you to express yourself clearly and exactly.
- It helps you to develop your writing style.
- It allows you to achieve a more fluent writing style.
- Examiners in GCSE English exams look for a range of sentence structures in your writing.
- It helps you to understand the correct use of the full range of punctuation marks and make the necessary checks at the end of any piece of writing.

What are the different types of sentence?
Sentence constructions can be:
- simple
- double
- multiple
- complex.

Simple sentences
- A simple sentence doesn't mean that the content is simple: it refers to the construction of the sentence.

▨ A simple sentence contains one verb and its subject.

Examples: Birds sing.
He walked to work.
My project will be finished soon.

▨ A simple sentence can vary in length. It doesn't always have to be very short.

Example: He walked five miles to work every day during the bus strike.

Double sentences
▨ Two simple sentences may be formed into one double sentence by joining them with *conjunctions*, or 'linking' words, such as **and, but, or.**

Examples: He likes tennis. He enjoys cricket. *(two simple sentences)*
He likes tennis and enjoys cricket. *(one double sentence)*

You will notice that the subject of the second simple sentence – **he** – has been left out. There is no need to repeat the subject as **he** is the subject of the first simple sentence.

Susan lives in Woking. She works in London. *(two simple sentences)*
Susan lives in Woking but works in London. *(one double sentence)*

▨ **And** is used to join closely related sentences:
The house was old **and** was beginning to fall down.

▨ **But** is used to join closely related sentences where a contrast is being made:
Tony says he is a vegetarian **but** he eats fish.

You can link sentences which don't have the same subject but they must make sense when joined together.

Example: **The weather** was wet. **We** went out for a walk.
/ \
subject *subject*

The weather was wet, but **we** went out for a walk.

Why use double sentences?

Read this holiday information about a Greek island.

> Have a wonderful time on Maxos. The sun always shines. It hardly ever rains. You can lie on sandy beaches. You can swim in crystal-clear seas. Food on Maxos is cheap. Wine is even cheaper. The people are friendly. They are always willing to talk to you about their island.

Because this passage is made up of several short, simple sentences and we pause at each full stop, the passage sounds disjointed. Compare the following passage with the passage above.

> Have a wonderful time on Maxos. The sun always shines and it hardly ever rains. You can lie on sandy beaches or swim in crystal-clear seas. Food on Maxos is cheap but wine is even cheaper. The people are friendly and are always willing to talk to you about their island.

By linking some of the sentences with **and, but, or,** the passage has lost some of its jerky style and sounds more fluent.

▨ Using double sentences in your writing helps you to vary your sentence length and achieve a more fluent style.

Multiple sentences

You have already seen that two sentences can be combined to make one. Sometimes three, or more, sentences can be linked together by using the conjunctions **and, but, or.**

Example: Len was waiting for Mary to return. He kept looking anxiously along the road. Mary did not appear.

Len was waiting for Mary to return **and** kept looking anxiously along the road **but** she did not appear.

▨ Three or more sentences can be linked together to form one sentence by using conjunctions. Sometimes words are omitted from the original sentences to avoid unnecessary repetition.

Complex sentences

▨ You can vary the length of the sentences you write by using double or multiple sentences. This makes your writing style more interesting.

▨ However, if you were to use only simple, double and multiple sentences, your writing would still appear rather tedious and stilted.

■ You should certainly avoid over-using words like **and** and **but**.

Example:

> 24 Redwood Way
> Dursley
> Glos.
> GL2 4RJ
> 20th September 1997
>
> Dear Giles,
> I hope you are well **and** enjoyed yourself at
> Christmas. We had a super time **and** now find it
> difficult to get back to the usual routine.
> Thank you very much for the presents you sent
> us. The children have played with the Scalextric
> for hours and hours **and** won't even stop for food!
> Paul has had a few attempts at it but he is really
> too young **and** usually ends up crashing his car
> **and** then there are tears **and** we have to divert
> him with other toys.

As you can see, **and** has frequently been used in this letter to link sentences
together. A greater variety of sentence constructions could help in creating a more
interesting style. For instance, instead of writing

> The children have played with the Scalextric for hours and hours and won't even
> stop for food!

you could write:

> The children, who have played with the Scalextric for hours and hours, won't even
> stop for food!

This type of sentence construction is called *complex*.

Example: When Mike phones, I shall tell him about the concert.

■ This sentence can be split into two parts (called *clauses*):
   ▶ *main* or *independent* clause
   ▶ *subordinate* or *dependent* clause.

I shall tell him about the concert. This is the *main* or *independent clause*:
it makes sense on its own and makes the main statement in the sentence.
When Mike phones, This is the *subordinate* or *dependent clause*:
it doesn't make sense on its own, but depends on the main clause to make sense.
Although **when** appears at the beginning of the sentence, it is the conjunction
that links the two parts of the sentence together.

Other examples:

The house **which** is owned by Councillor Oddy is for sale.

main clause   *subordinate clause*   *main clause continued*

Reisa is always late **because** she never wears a watch.

main clause   *subordinate clause*

The link words are shown in bold type.

- A complex sentence will always have at least one main clause.
- It may have more than one dependent clause.

The boy, **who** was called Tom, fell asleep at once, **as** he was very tired.

main clause   *first subordinate clause*   *main clause continued*   *second subordinate clause*

Although we warned her, Ivy forgot to close her door **before** the rain started.

first subordinate clause   *main clause*   *second subordinate clause*

- There are many words that can be used as conjunctions in complex sentences, for instance:

when	which	because	who	although	before	since
if	after	where	until	unless	than	while	as

Checkpoints

- Use a variety of constructions in your writing. It makes it more interesting and fluent.
- Always check your work to make sure you haven't:
  - used too many short, jerky sentences
  - joined too many ideas together with **and**.

  If you have, then consider other ways of constructing your sentences.
- Don't assume that long, complicated sentences are always best and only use these. There is also a place for simple sentences. They can be very effective.
- The important thing is to express your ideas clearly and to vary your sentence structure.

4 Capital Letters

Different languages use capital letters for different reasons.

In English we use capital letters to begin each day of the week, whereas in Spanish and French days of the week all begin with a small (lower-case) letter. We use capital letters for proper nouns in English, but in German capital letters are used for all nouns, so that **snow** (der Schnee) in German needs a capital **S** whereas in English we write **snow** with a small **s**.

- Knowing about the use of capital letters is an important part of knowing about a language.
- In present day English there are clear reasons for using capital letters, and only in some instances does personal preference prevail.

In this chapter we refer to several *parts of speech*: *personal pronouns*, *proper nouns* and *adjectives*. If you are uncertain about the meaning of any of them, turn to the relevant chapters in the *Grammar* section of this book.

What are capital letters used for?

Capital letters are used:

- to begin every sentence
- for the pronoun **I**
- for proper names (proper nouns)
- for titles
- for days of the weeks, months of the year and festivals
- in letters
- to begin a line of poetry.

Why is it important to know about them?

- They are conventions of standard English.
- In GCSE English you can lose marks if you fail to use capital letters or use them for the wrong reasons.

Beginning sentences

▨ A sentence always begins with a capital letter.

You are probably quite aware that every sentence you write must begin with a capital letter. It isn't a problem to remember this: the main dilemma about sentences is understanding what a sentence is and knowing when one ends and the next begins.

▨ When speech is written, each new sentence requires a capital letter at the beginning. This applies whether the dialogue is part of a passage or part of a play.

Examples: Maxine blinked feebly. She felt hands tugging gently at her shoulders. A bright light was being held close to her face and she could hear the sound of muffled voices above the roar of machinery. 'Leave me. I'm sleepy and my legs hurt,' she whispered.

HARRY	I couldn't believe my luck. It's not often you find a £20 note lying in the gutter just waiting to be picked up. It was outside the sheltered housing scheme in Duke Street.
SHEILA	Did you take it to the police or give it to the warden at Meadowvale?
HARRY	Neither, love. I pocketed it. Anyone careless enough to drop this obviously can afford to lose it. Think what it will buy us at the take-away.
SHEILA	I'm not helping you spend it. Please, Harry, hand it in.

▨ At times speech is made up of one-word answers, partly finished sentences or phrases. Despite this, the first word still needs a capital letter even though it isn't a sentence.

Example:
STUART	Hungry?
JASON	Not really.
STUART	Coke?
JASON	Cheers!
MATTHEW	Nobody asked ...
STUART	Sorry, mate!

The pronoun I

▨ A capital letter is used for the personal pronoun I, regardless of where the word occurs in a sentence.

▨ There are no exceptions to the rule.

Examples: I haven't made up my mind who to vote for yet.
In May, I am going to walk the four highest peaks in the British Isles.

- I stands instead of your name. You would use a capital letter for your name.
- When I is linked to another word to make a shortened form (a *contraction*), it still needs a capital letter.

Examples: I'm (I am)   I'll (I will)
           I'd (I should/would) I've (I have)

(To find out more about contractions, see Chapter 10 *Apostrophes*.)

Proper names (proper nouns)
place names

our names

nationalities and languages

other names

Place names

house name	Winton
road	4 Auckland Avenue
district	Nettlecombe
town	Stone
county	Staffs
postcode	ST1 5ST
country	England

- Other place names, such as particular hamlets, villages, continents, oceans, rivers, lakes, deserts, glaciers or mountains, need a capital letter at the beginning:

River Trent Arctic Ocean Kalahari Desert

- As these are the names of a particular river, ocean and desert, both words in the place name need a capital letter at the beginning.
- However, when words such as **river, ocean, mountain, desert** and **glacier** are being used in general terms, and not as the name of any particular place, then no capital letter is needed at the beginning:

I enjoy a picnic by a river.
The water in the lake flowed from the glaciers above.
It can be bitterly cold in deserts at night.

Our names
- Whenever you write your own first name(s) or surname, you use a capital letter at the beginning. This applies to everyone, so all forenames and surnames need a capital letter at the beginning.

    Examples: Tony Blair   Alan Shearer   Chris Evans

- This rule also applies to the names of pets, fictional characters and nicknames.

    Examples: Rover   Winnie the Pooh   Ginger

Nationalities and languages
- You have already seen that towns, countries and continents need an initial capital letter: so do the people who live in them.

    Examples: Manchester → Mancunians   Portugal → Portuguese
               Europe → Europeans

- The languages spoken throughout the world all need to begin with a capital letter.

    Examples: Italian   Japanese   Russian

- *Adjectives* are describing words which describe nouns or pronouns. Adjectives can be made from proper nouns. Such adjectives, unlike others, need an initial capital letter.

Examples:	**proper noun**	**adjective made from noun**
	Dickens (name of author)	a **Dickensian** character
	Elizabeth (name of queen)	the **Elizabethan** era
	Colombia (name of country)	a **Colombian** runner
	Glasgow (name of town)	a **Glaswegian** comedian

Other names
- Initial capital letters are also used for important or particular:

buildings	ships	makes of cars/aeroplanes
brand names	firms	words connected with religions
organisations	political parties or theories	

Examples:	Tower of London	Tewkesbury Abbey	York Cathedral
	Hull University	Foreign Office	Ford Mondeo
	Marks & Spencers	Heinz	Allah
	Bible	Republicans	Weetabix
	S.S. Titanic	H.M.S. Fearless	European Union
	Concorde	Orient Express	Tesco
	National Trust	Liberal Democrats	Communism

Titles

People

▨ Each of us has a title which must begin with a capital letter.

Examples: **M**iss Rutherford **M**r Upright **M**rs Boyd **M**s Johnson **U**ncle Ian
Lord Archer **D**octor Kassam **R**everend Higgins **I**nspector Morse

▨ Titles begin with a capital letter when they are used with a person's name, but they only require small letters when they are used in other ways.

Examples: All their mothers and fathers were invited.
Three of my aunts and two of my uncles are going to the wedding.
The foreign secretaries of all nine countries were at the meeting.

Other titles

| books | plays | poems | television and radio programmes |
| films | songs | special events | newspapers and magazines |

▨ In titles such as these, the first word and all the important words within the title begin with a capital letter; less important words are given a small letter.

Examples: **Of M**ice and **M**en **M**uch **A**do **A**bout **N**othing **H**aunted
Remains of the **D**ay **T**rooping of the **C**olour **D**aily **M**irror

Days, months and festivals

▨ All days of the week, months of the year and special festivals begin with capital letters.

Examples: **W**ednesday **A**pril 23rd **B**ank **H**oliday **M**onday **R**amadan **B**oxing **D**ay

Letters

▨ In letters the greeting **Dear** begins with a capital letter, as do **Sir** and **Madam** when they form the greeting **Dear Sir** or **Dear Madam**.

▨ The first word after the greeting needs a capital letter:

Dear **P**aula,

Thank you for a most ...

▨ The first letter of the closing phrase also needs a capital letter:

With love
Yours sincerely
Yours faithfully

Lines of poetry
- In poetry (with a few modern exceptions) each line begins with a capital letter:

When you are old and grey and full of sleep,
And nodding by the fire, take down this book,
And slowly read, and dream of the soft look
Your eyes had once, and of their shadows deep;

—from *When You Are Old* by W.B. Yeats

Do you need capital letters?
Problems can occur with certain words that are used in one instance with a capital letter and in another without. Remember this guideline.

Use a capital letter for the specific and a small letter for the general.

Examples: The **B**oard meets on the first Friday of every month.
Every company has a **b**oard of directors.

Rudhill High **S**chool has an excellent exam record.
All **s**chools in the area were closed during the floods.

Checkpoints
- Try to remember the list of the main reasons for using capital letters given on the first page of this chapter.
- There is a great deal of information in this chapter, so go back over any points that you are uncertain about.
- Use this chapter as a reference source when you are checking your work for capital letters.

5 Full Stops

What are full stops used for?

Full stops are used:

- at the ends of sentences
- for abbreviations and initials.

Sentence enders

- A full stop is used at the end of every *statement* sentence and at the end of some *command* sentences. (Others end in an exclamation mark – see Chapter 7.)

Statement sentences

As you saw in Chapter 2, a statement sentence expresses a fact or opinion.

Examples: The disco was closed. *(fact)*
Anna is a very pleasant person. *(opinion)*

Statement sentences make up most of our speech and writing.

Command sentences

These are used more in speech than writing, as we are more likely to give a command when we are talking to someone than when we write. However, you may write commands as part of a set of instructions or as part of a passage of direct speech.

Examples: Place the A4 paper in the lower tray.
Lever the tyre away from the rim.

'Sit on the side of the bath first.'
'Move the papers.'

As the last two dialogue sentence end in full stops, we assume they are said in an advisory way. If, as a writer, you want to show that someone is saying something with strong feeling or emotion then you should end your command with an exclamation mark (see Chapter 7).

Example: 'Help me get rid of the evidence!'

Initial letters
▨ It is usual to put a full stop after each initial letter of:
 ▶ a person's name
 ▶ a company's name
 ▶ an organisation's name
 ▶ an accepted abbreviation

Examples   D. Hill – Damon Hill
P.D. James – Phyllis Dorothy James
I.T.N. – Independent Television News
C.A.B. – Citizens' Advice Bureau
P.T.O. – Please turn over
D.I.Y. – Do-it-yourself

Abbreviations
These are commonly used in telephone directories, dictionaries, advertisements, addresses, etc., where we want to give information in a limited space.

Examples: in dictionaries – v. colloq. sing. abbrev. Fr. pro. Lat.
in addresses – Cres. Cambs. Sq. Lincs. Glos.

Not all abbreviated words have a full stop after them.

Example:

> Peugeot 506 – H
> reg. 570,000 miles,
> ex. cond., 1300
> c.c., 6 mnths MOT,
> £3000 o.n.o.

▨ A full stop is generally placed after the last letter of an abbreviation if that last letter is different from the last letter of the complete word, e.g. 'ex. cond.' for 'excellent condition'.

▨ There is a trend for missing out full stops after abbreviations regardless of the guideline above. It is also becoming increasingly popular to miss out the full stops after initial letters. You will see them written both ways.

▨ Metric abbreviations don't need full stops after them.

l	(litre/s)	mm	millimetre
g	(gram/s)	cm	(centimetre/s)
kg	(kilogram/s)	km	(kilometre/s)

Checkpoints

- Follow the guidelines, but remember you may not always see the guidelines being followed for initials and abbreviations.
- A full stop should always be used at the end of a statement sentence and some commands.

6 Question Marks

What are question marks used for?

- A question mark is used to replace the full stop at the end of a sentence that asks a question. No full stop is needed.

  Examples: Why are you always complaining?
  Where did you put Mr and Mrs Major's file?
  Which character in the play is most likely to evoke the reader's sympathy?
  Do you think this poet creates a more vivid picture of the harvest?
  Can you persuade Peter to join us?

- Questions can also appear within quoted dialogue, in which case the question mark is always placed within the quotation marks (see Chapter 11 *Quotation Marks*).

  'Which man do you most admire?' she whispered.

What are the different types of question?

A question can be:

- direct
- rhetorical.

Direct questions

- A *direct question* is one that requires an answer. Direct questions can be classed as *closed questions* or *open questions*.
- A *closed question* expects the answer **yes** or **no**.

  Examples: Is Amanda a member?
  Do spiders feel pain?

- An *open question* requires more than **yes** or **no** as an answer. Open questions usually begin with one of the question words **where**, **when**, **how**, **why**, **which**, **what** or **who**.

Examples: Why did the Romans invade Britain?
What is the meaning of 'orthodontics'?

▨ Avoid asking direct questions in formal letters, essays or reports. Try to replace the question with a statement:

Will you send me further details, please?

could be replaced by

I would be grateful if you could send me further details.

Rhetorical questions

▨ These are questions that do not require an answer.

For example, a headmaster addressing pupils in assembly may say:

How can we improve the situation?

He may well not pause for the pupils or staff to answer, but go on to tell his audience exactly what he thinks they can do to improve the situation.

Speakers addressing an audience often ask a question without expecting their audience to answer. They may even feel annoyed if someone interrupts and answers their question.

Checkpoints

▨ Make sure that you can distinguish between a question and a statement.

He wondered where everyone had disappeared to.

This is a statement that reports on his thoughts. It isn't the same as:

'Where has everyone disappeared to?' he wondered.

▨ In formal writing activities, only use direct questions as part of dialogue.

---

7 Exclamation Marks

What are exclamation marks used for?

An exclamation mark is used to replace the full stop at the end of:

- exclamatory sentences
- brief, forceful commands
- interjections.

Exclamatory sentences

- As you saw in Chapter 2, you need an exclamation mark at the end of an exclamatory sentence. Such sentences convey emotion, for instance anger, pleasure or sadness.

  Examples: What a terrible mistake he made!
  How kind of him to ask!

- It is possible to confuse an exclamatory sentence with a question when it begins with **what** or **how**.

  Examples: What do you think? *(question)*
  What a beautiful dog he is! *(exclamation)*
  How do you know? *(question)*
  How upsetting for you to lose! *(exclamation)*

If you find it difficult to decide between using a question mark and an exclamation mark, ask yourself:

Is a question being asked?

Does the sentence require an answer?

If the answer is 'yes' to both these questions, then you need a question mark.

Brief commands

- Commands don't always end in an exclamation mark. You saw in Chapter 2 that a command can end in a full stop.

  Example: Add the flour.

- If the command needs to be said forcefully, then end it with an exclamation mark.

    Examples: Be quiet!
    Run away!
    Sit here!
    Don't light the fuse!

Interjections
- Interjections are words which express an emotion.
- They are more often used in speech than in writing but you may use them as part of a dialogue.

    Examples: Damn! Ouch! Gadzooks! Here, here! Oyez, oyez! Oho! Cor!
    'Ah! Now I understand,' Tom cried in triumph.

When you are writing dialogue, it is possible to punctuate certain sentences in two ways. Either is correct.

    Example: 'Ah! Now I understand,' Tom cried in triumph.

The exclamation mark is placed after the interjection **Ah!**, followed by a separate sentence.

    'Ah, now I understand!' Tom cried in triumph.

This has now been made into one sentence. A comma has been placed after the interjection and the exclamation mark appears at the end of the sentence.

Checkpoints
- An exclamation mark doesn't need a full stop after it. It replaces a full stop.
- Do not pepper your writing with exclamation marks. They serve a specific purpose, as we have outlined in this chapter.

8 Commas

What is a comma?

- A comma is used within a sentence to separate one group of words from another so that the meaning of the sentence is clear.
- A comma signals to the reader that he or she should pause briefly.

Why are commas important?

- Commas placed in the correct position for the right reasons help your readers to make sense of your writing.
- The inclusion and position of commas can make all the difference to the meaning of a sentence.

Here are two sentences with the same words in them, but the inclusion of commas gives each a different meaning.

'Becky, our secretary has left us.'
'Becky, our secretary, has left us.'

In the first sentence we pause after **Becky** as we read the sentence. We are talking to Becky and telling her about our secretary.

In the second sentence we pause after **Becky** and again after **secretary**. This makes us realise that Becky is the secretary who has just left.

What are commas used for?

We use commas:

- in lists
- for dates and numbers
- in letters and addresses
- in dialogue and quotations.

Commas in lists

items	actions
groups of words	adverbs
adjectives	

A list of items

Examples: I bought a pair of earrings, some shampoo, a pair of tights and some perfume.

Alex doesn't eat pork, beef, lamb or ham.

- In both sentences the items in the list are separated from one another by a comma.
- Commas in a list help you, at a glance, to sort one item from another and make sense of the list.
- There is no need for a comma before the last item in each list, as it is separated from the previous item by a conjunction.
- There are occasions when it is helpful to place a comma before a conjunction at the end of a list.

Example: On their sponsored pub crawl they visited the Slug and Lettuce, the Crown and Anchor, the Pig and Whistle, and the Fox and Hounds.

Visually the final comma helps to separate one pub from another and stops any confusion arising.

A list of groups

- The items in a list don't have to be single words: they can be groups of words.

Example: The sixth-former wore jeans with wide turn-ups, a white shirt with a crumpled collar, a baseball cap with the peak turned to the side and trainers.

A list of adjectives

- When several adjectives are listed in a sentence, they are usually separated by commas (see Chapter 18 *Adjectives*).

Examples: Her latest partner is **clever, handsome** and **rich**.

Sally's **long, slim, elegant** silhouette made her smile with pleasure.

The adjectives may appear *after* the noun that they describe and separated from the noun (as in the first sentence), or *before* the noun (second sentence).

- Each adjective should be separated by a comma.
- You don't need a comma between the final adjective and the noun it describes (second sentence).
- If adjectives go together fluently and describe one another then no comma is needed.

Example: He was wearing a **pale blue** suit and **dark pink** shirt.

A list of actions

Examples: Each evening in summer my father waters the garden, walks the dog and then sits under the plum tree.

The demonstrators shouted, swore and waved their fists.

■ The actions can be single words or groups of words. Each is separated from the next by a comma unless there is a conjunction to separate the actions.

A list of adverbs

■ Adverbs give us more information about verbs (see Chapter 19 *Adverbs*). When a list of adverbs appear together in a sentence, each adverb is separated by a comma.

Examples: Suzie ate her food slowly, shyly and delicately.

Slowly, shyly and **delicately** are the adverbs which give more information about the verb **ate**.

Commas for dates and numbers

■ You can choose to include commas in dates or you can omit them. You will see them written both ways. The choice is yours.

Example: May 4th, 1997 *or* May 4th 1997

■ In numbers it is helpful if you place a comma after each group of three figures. The number is then easier to read.

Example: 689,000 1,000,000 3,645

■ When you write a sentence, it can help if you use a comma to separate certain numbers, to make it easier for your readers.

Example: On January 3rd 1945, 178 people were injured in a landslide.

Commas in letters and addresses

50 Edgehill Road,
Greens Borton,
Nr Towcester,
Northants.
NN2 3ER

■ In a handwritten letter, it is still common to put a comma after each line of the address, except the last line (before the postcode) which needs a full stop. You will notice that each line is indented so that the address is sloping.

■ However, it is becoming increasingly popular to 'block' addresses (to use no indentations), and to leave out all punctuation. This style is always used with typed correspondence.

```
50 Edgehill Road
Greens Borton
Nr Towcester
Northants
NN2 3ER
```

For general use it doesn't matter which you choose, but you must be consistent. For exam purposes it is advisable to indent and correctly punctuate addresses when you write formal letters to show that you understand the conventions.

■ If you write an address along a line, for example as part of a letter, you should use commas to separate each item in the address. Visually it is easier to read:

50 Edgehill Road, Greens Borton, Nr Towcester, Northants. NN2 3ER

■ In a handwritten letter a comma is needed after the name of the person you are sending the letter to:

Dear Sir, Dear Miss Winter, Dear Rebecca,

■ A comma is also needed after the last word of the final greeting:

Yours faithfully, With love, Yours sincerely,

■ In typed letters these commas are left out.

Commas in dialogue and quotations

(There is more about using dialogue and quotations in Chapter 11 *Quotation Marks*.)

Commas are used:

■ to introduce quotations
■ to separate dialogue from the rest of a sentence
■ when you are addressing someone
■ when **yes** or **no** form part of an answer
■ in interjections, some questions and asides.

To introduce quotations

■ When we use the words that someone said or wrote, we use a comma to introduce the quotation. This happens in both dialogue and prose passages.

Examples: The Hansom Report stated, 'If action is not taken within the next month to improve the water supply to the camp, many refugees will die from disease.'

Aunt Anna's favourite saying was, 'Live and let live.'

To separate dialogue from the rest of a sentence

Examples: Charlotte pleaded, 'Please come with me tonight!'

'Give him a nudge,' whispered Tony.

'Find a seat first,' suggested Michael, 'and then I'll order.'

In these examples the actual words spoken (in quotation marks) are separated from the rest of each sentence by a comma.

When you are addressing someone
- When you address someone, you should separate their name from the rest of the sentence by one or more commas.
- When we speak, we pause before and after the name of the person we are speaking to. By naming the person, we interrupt the flow of the sentence. The comma or commas mark the interruption.

Examples: 'I expect, Jill, that you are looking forward to starting your new job,' Amie said.

'Pete, do you always make so much noise when you drink?' Melanie enquired.

'I know you want to go to Prague this summer, Harry,' Shula announced.

- If you are talking *about* a person and not *to* them, you don't need a comma.

Example: 'I met Toby in the town yesterday.'

When *yes* or *no* form part of an answer

Examples: 'No, I can't join you.'
'Yes, count me in.'

- The **yes** and **no** interrupt the flow of each sentence and a comma is used to show this pause.
- If **no** isn't used as part of an answer in dialogue, it doesn't need a comma after it.

Examples: 'There is no more room,' replied Brian.

'No material can beat it,' the salesman boasted.

In interjections, some questions and asides
(If you are uncertain about *interjections*, see Chapter 7, page 25.)

> *interjection*   'Oh, how dreadful for him!'

■ The interjection **oh** is acting as an aside at the beginning of the sentence and needs a comma after it. If you say the sentence aloud, you will notice how you pause after **oh**.

> *asides*   'Naturally, he'll come first.'   or   'He'll come first, naturally.'
> 'Obviously, she's in love again.'   or   'She's in love again, obviously.'

■ We often use asides in conversation. Remember to use a comma to separate an aside.

> *questions*   'Nice mess you got me into, didn't you?'
> 'You'll come, won't you?'

■ In conversation we frequently add a question clause. A comma is used to separate the question part of the sentence.

Checkpoints

■ In this chapter you have looked at using commas for lists, dates, numbers, addresses, letters, dialogue and quotations.

■ The reasons for using commas are quite straightforward: it is a case of remembering the reasons and practising.

■ In the next chapter you will look at how commas are used in complex sentences.

■ Look carefully at how other writers use commas, as this will help you to remember the points that you have learnt in this chapter.

9 More Uses for Commas

What are the other uses for commas?

We use commas:
- for subordinate clauses
- with conjunctions
- for asides
- for sense.

Understanding sentences

In Chapter 3 *More Sentences*, you were introduced to:
- complex sentences
- main clauses
- subordinate clauses.

Revision points

- A *main clause* or *independent clause* is the main part of a sentence. It makes sense and can stand alone.
- A *subordinate clause* or *dependent clause* gives more information about the main clause. It can't stand alone as it doesn't make sense by itself.

If there are any other points you are uncertain about as you work through this chapter, turn back to Chapter 3.

Commas for subordinate clauses

Examples: If we have the day off, I will go to the computer exhibition.

subordinate clause comma   main clause

After the optician examined her, he said she would need glasses.

subordinate clause   comma   main clause

- When the subordinate clause occurs at the beginning of a sentence, it is usual to use a comma to separate it from the main clause.

■ It is particularly helpful to do this when the subordinate clause is very long.

Example: subordinate clause [After he attended a long tutorial session
                                 [to discuss his plans for the future,
          main clause   [he decided to join the Royal Navy.

If you read the last sentence aloud, you will probably notice that you paused after the word **future**. The comma marks this pause.

■ If the subordinate clause is at the end of a sentence, you don't have to use a comma to separate it from the main clause.

Example: I would like to go to the computer exhibition if we have the day off.

               main clause   subordinate clause

Commas with conjunctions

■ In Chapter 3 you saw that a comma is usually unnecessary when either **and** or **or** is used to join two parts of a sentence together.

Example: Arif is a prefect and enjoys the responsibility.

The conjunction **and** joins the two parts of this sentence together. No comma is needed.

■ It is often helpful to use a comma before the conjunction **but**. It can help to create a contrast.

Example: The caretaker always works hard polishing the floors, but he does not enjoy doing it.

■ You can use a comma with other conjunctions too if you want to emphasise a point.

Example: I will write the essay again, although I don't think I can improve it.

■ A comma also helps if the sentence is very long.

Example: Tests have proved that Simon is allergic to a large variety of everyday substances, and anti-histamine tablets have not helped him in any way.

■ When there is a different subject in each clause in a sentence, a comma after the conjunction can be useful.

Example: Andy played the violin, and Jacob played the tuba.

Andy is the subject of the first part of the sentence; Jacob is the subject of the second part.

Commas for asides

Examples: Mrs McKenzie, my brother's mother-in-law, has won the lottery.

This gives you extra information about Mrs McKenzie.

Our holiday, the first one for four years, was a disaster.

If you remove this extra information, the sentence would still make sense.

Clive has, to my knowledge, been caught three times.

This is an aside.

- In all of these examples, the bracketed words are asides. They give some extra information, but they are not essential to the meaning of the sentence. If you removed each aside, you would still have a sentence which makes sense.
- Each aside has been divided from the rest of the sentence by commas. The commas act like a pair of brackets showing that the words within them are less important than the rest of the sentence. This helps the reader to read and understand the sentence.
- You can always test whether you have used commas correctly for asides. If you remove the aside, you should still have a complete sentence.
- An aside can also be placed at the beginning or end of a sentence.

Examples: Generally speaking, these plants can tolerate quite low temperatures.
I hate French, all things considered.

Common mistakes
- Sometimes commas are placed around words which aren't an aside but an essential part of the sentence.

Examples: The teacher **at the head of the queue** is responsible for organising the school trip.

That boy **wearing the black leather jacket** used to go to my last school.

The first prize goes to the man **standing in front of the projector**.

The painting **which is on the wall outside the chemistry laboratory** is mine.

The words in bold type in each sentence above are essential to the meaning of the sentence. They do not need commas around them as they aren't asides.
at the head of the queue tells you which teacher is organising the trip.

wearing the black leather jacket defines which boy it is.

You identify your painting by the words **which is on the wall outside the chemistry laboratory.**

You wouldn't know which man won the prize if you removed **standing in front of the projector.**

▨ The bold words are called *defining clauses*: they point out which person or thing is being referred to.

Commas for sense

▨ A comma can make all the difference to the meaning of a sentence.

Examples: He knows I believe she is innocent. *(I believe she is innocent.)*
He knows, I believe, she is innocent. *(He knows she is innocent.)*

He left us to go surfing. *(We go surfing.)*
He left us, to go surfing. *(He goes surfing.)*

▨ A sentence can be confusing if commas have been left out or used incorrectly.

Examples: According to Sue Johnson is guilty. *(It doesn't make sense.)*
According to Sue, Johnson is guilty. *(It now makes sense.)*

He drove to the vet's with his girlfriend and his hamster in the cage.
(Did his girlfriend enjoy being in the cage with the hamster?)

He drove to the vet's with his girlfriend, and his hamster in the cage.
(Now his girlfriend doesn't have to share the hamster's cage.)

He carried the plate and the plums in wine into the dining room.
(A new recipe – 'plate and plums in wine'?)

He carried the plate, and the plums in wine into the dining room.
(He is now carrying two separate items.)

Checkpoints

- It is important to be able to identify the main and subordinate clauses in sentences. You can then check that you have used commas correctly.

- A comma represents a short pause and helps your reader make sense of your writing.

- It is particularly important to use commas correctly to break up longer or more complicated sentences so that they can be more easily understood.

- Examiners in GCSE English will wish to see that you can use commas correctly.

- If you miss out a comma or commas, put them in unnecessarily or in the wrong place, you can alter the meaning of what you want to say and confuse your reader.

- Learn the rules for using commas but also use your common sense.

10 Apostrophes

What is an apostrophe?

■ An apostrophe is a raised comma '.

What are apostrophes used for?

■ An apostrophe is used to show that a letter or letters have been missed out of a word. Words shortened in this way are called *contractions*.

■ It is used with nouns to show ownership. (See Chapter 15 *Nouns* to find out more about nouns.)

Why are apostrophes important?

■ They serve a particular purpose and give information to people reading your writing.

■ Examiners of GCSE English papers frequently comment on the misuse or absence of apostrophes.

■ Apostrophes aren't difficult to use. There are clear guidelines for their use and if you understand the basic uses, you shouldn't have any problems.

Apostrophes for contractions

I'm (I am) I've (I have) I'll (I will/shall) I'd (I would/should) we're (we are)
you've (you have) we'll (we will/shall) he's (he is/has) she's (she is/has)
it's (it is/has) they're (they are) where's (where is) there's (there is) isn't (is not)
aren't (are not) can't (cannot) shouldn't (should not) wouldn't (would not)
6 o'clock (6 of the clock) sou'wester (south west gale or special rain hat)

■ In each of these words an apostrophe has been used to show that one or more letters have been missed out.

■ In **shan't** (short for 'shall not') and **won't** (short for 'will not'), the spelling of the original words has altered.

■ An apostrophe that indicates a missing letter can also be added to a noun:
The dinner's ready. *(The dinner is ready.)*

The **i** of **is** has been omitted and an apostrophe has been used to replace it.

- An apostrophe is often used to indicate a missing number:

    He visited the States in '73. *(He visited the States in 1973.)*

The apostrophe has been used to show that **19** is missing.

- An apostrophe is also used in dialogue to show when someone speaking in a particular accent is missing out letters:

    "E 'ad a 'eadache.' *('He had a headache')*

Here an apostrophe has been used for each missing **h** at the beginning of words.

- We often use contractions in speech. It is something you may write in dialogue so that your characters sound authentic, but you should normally avoid such contractions in formal writing.

Apostrophes to show ownership

Examples: the **secretary's** filofax
                 her **husband's** socks
                 the **cat's** fur
                 Philip's birthday
                 a **bird's** feather
                 Gill's ankle
                 the **machine's** manual
                 the **judge's** wig

The words in bold type are the owners.

- In each case there is one owner, and an apostrophe has been placed after the owner's name and an **s** added after it. This shows the reader that something is owned.

    It is the birthday of Philip (**Philip's** birthday).

    It is the wig of the judge (the **judge's** wig).

> **Remember**
> - If there is one owner:
>   - write the word for the owner
>   - place an apostrophe after it
>   - add s.
> - If there is *one* owner, the apostrophe must go *before* the s.

Now we will look at what happens when there is more than one owner.

Examples: all the **teachers'** cars
the **twins'** mother
several **dogs'** collars
those **candidates'** papers
seven **pupils'** books
the two **girls'** relations
the **assistants'** uniform
these **employees'** files

The words in bold type are the owners.

In each case there is more than one owner, so the word ends in s. An apostrophe has been placed after this final s. No additional s has been added – it is unnecessary.

Remember

▨ If there is *more than one* owner (the owner is *plural*):

  ◗ write the plural word for the owners (ending in s)

  ◗ place an apostrophe at the end of the word after this final s.

▨ If there is *more than one* owner, the apostrophe must go *after* the s.

Possessive pronouns

▨ The words in the examples for the owner or owners have all been nouns (see Chapter 15). You only add an apostrophe to a noun to show ownership. Possessive pronouns such as

mine yours his hers ours theirs

are never used with an apostrophe (see Chapter 16).

Implied possessions

▨ Sometimes we leave out the word that is being owned.

Examples: The **baker's** is at the end of our road. *(baker's shop)*
I'm going to **Sam's** after school. *(Sam's house)*

We often leave out the words **home**, **house** or **flat**, and just put the name of the person, followed by an apostrophe and an s to show ownership.

Possessives of irregular plurals
- There are certain plurals that don't seem to obey the rule for using apostrophes.

Examples: children's women's men's

Unlike most plural nouns, **children, women** and **men** don't end in an s, so it is necessary to add an s *after* the apostrophe.

> **Remember**
> - If there is a plural owner *not* ending in s:
>   - write the word for the owner
>   - place an apostrophe after it
>   - add s.

- The same thing happens with words that are the same in their singular and plural forms, for instance **deer, salmon.**

Examples: The **deer's** predators are many.
This stretch of river is the **salmon's** favourite haunt.

Possessives of compound nouns
- In compound words such as:

mother-in-law father-in-law

an apostrophe is added to the last part of the word to show ownership.

Example: My **mother-in-law's** brother is my next-door neighbour.

Possessives of names ending in *s*
- When people's names end in s, you have a choice:
  - write the word and put an apostrophe after it

Giles' bedroom **Mr Mates'** plants

  - write the word, put an apostrophe after it and then add s.

Giles's bedroom **Mr Mates's** plants
- This rule only applies to names. It doesn't apply to common nouns that end in s or ss.

Examples: *atlas* You have torn the new **atlas's** cover.
witness The jury didn't believe the **witness's** story.

Expressions of time
- Many expressions of time need an apostrophe:

  one day's pay   a month's holiday   three weeks' work
- If the period of time is *singular* (**one day**), put an apostrophe at the end of the word and then add **s**.
- If the period of time is *plural* (**three weeks**), write the word and put an apostrophe after the final **s** of the word.

Common mistakes

It's and *its*
- Its shows ownership.

  Examples: You can't borrow my bike because **its** tyres are flat.

- It's with an apostrophe is short for **it is**

  Examples: **It's** the first day off I've had for six weeks.

There's and *theirs*
These words are spelt differently, but sound the same and can be confused.
- Theirs shows ownership.

  Examples: The new leather bags by the locker are **theirs**.

- There's is the shortened form of **there is**

  Examples: I can't see if **there's** a ship on the horizon or not.

Who's and *whose*
- Whose indicates ownership.

  Examples: Enrico didn't know **whose** clothes they were.

- Who's is short for **who is**

  Examples: **Who's** that man in the dark glasses?

Checkpoints

- Apostrophes are easy to use if you understand the rules.
- Learn the rules and put them into practice. If you are ever uncertain, come back to this chapter and check.
- Words that are shortened need an apostrophe to show that a letter or letters are missing. These contractions should normally only be used for informal situations and dialogue.
- Apostrophes to show ownership are only added to nouns.
- If there is one owner, add an apostrophe at the end of the word and then add **s**.
- If there is more than one owner, ending in **s**, write the word and then add an apostrophe.
- Remember the common words that are a special case: **women's, men's** and **children's**.

11 Quotation Marks

What are quotation marks?

- These punctuation marks consist of sets of double (" ") or single (' ') raised commas, of which the first comma, or pair of commas, is *inverted* (upside-down).
- They are placed around words to show that they are taken from spoken dialogue or from another piece of writing.
- You can use either double or single quotation marks, although printed books (such as this one) more commonly use the single form. If you like, you can use double quotation marks for dialogue and single quotation marks for other quotations.
- Quotation marks are also referred to as *speech marks* or *inverted commas*.

Why are quotation marks important?

- They show your reader that you are using dialogue or quoting from another source.
- They are an accepted part of punctuation, and examiners in GCSE English exams expect you to be able to use them correctly.
- In other subjects at GCSE you will also often need to include quotations as part of your writing.

What are quotation marks used for?

Quotation marks are used for:
- direct speech or dialogue
- other quotations.

Direct speech

▩ There are two ways of expressing speech:
  ▶ indirect or reported speech
  ▶ direct speech.

Examples: Mrs Mitchell said that she ordered the books last Friday. *(indirect speech)*

Mrs Mitchell said, 'I ordered the books last Friday.' *(direct speech)*

In the second example you read the exact words that Mrs Mitchell said, whereas the first example conveys the content of the dialogue without quoting the exact words that Mrs Mitchell used.

▩ When the actual words a speaker uses are written down, quotation marks separate them from the rest of the sentence.

▩ Sentences containing direct speech can be structured in various ways.

'Have you tried paintballing?' asked Josh.
  words spoken   *speaker*

Elizabeth announced excitedly, 'I've got the job!'
  speaker   *words spoken*

'The litter is appalling,' said Mr Fry, 'and we have to do something about it.'
  words spoken   *speaker*   *continuation of words spoken*

'I must go now,' Hazel replied. 'I can't be late for geography again.'
  words spoken   *speaker*   *words spoken (new speech sentence)*

▩ The words spoken are always enclosed within quotation marks.

▩ The words within the quotation marks are separated from the rest of the sentence by a comma, question mark or exclamation mark.

Examples: 'I want to see Mr Newing now,' the customer demanded. *(statement)*
'Have you lived there long?' the receptionist enquired. *(question)*
'What a day!' Richard complained. *(exclamation)*

▩ When you use a question mark or exclamation mark, you don't need a comma.

▩ Final punctuation marks – question marks, exclamation marks or full stops – associated with the words spoken should be placed within the quotation marks.

These sentences could equally well have been written with the speaker first.

Examples: The customer demanded, 'I want to see Mr Newing now.' *(statement)*
The receptionist enquired, 'Have you lived there long?' *(question)*
Richard complained, 'What a day!' *(exclamation)*

44

■ Here a comma is used before the words spoken to separate them from the rest of the sentence.

■ The first word of speech always starts with a capital letter, except when a sentence is interrupted.

Example: 'If you walk too far,' Colin said, 'you'll be exhausted.'

     capital letter   interruption   lower-case letter

It is sometimes difficult to decide whether there is an interruption or two separate sentences. To avoid making a mistake, remove the interruption:

'If you walk too far, you'll be exhausted.'

If the two parts make sense together then it is one sentence, and you need a lower-case letter for the first word in the quotation marks after the interruption.

■ When you write a piece of dialogue, you should begin each speaker's contribution on a new line. This helps your readers to follow the conversation.

■ You place quotation marks around whole groups of uninterrupted speech sentences and not around each separate sentence.

Example: 'Third boy, what's a horse?'
'A beast, sir,' replied the boy.
'So it is,' said Squeers. 'Ain't it, Nickleby?'
'I believe there is no doubt of that, sir,' answered Nicholas.
'Of course there isn't,' said Squeers. 'A horse is a quadruped, and quadruped's Latin for beast, as everybody that's gone through the grammar knows, or else where's the use of having grammar at all?'

—from *Nicholas Nickleby* by **Charles Dickens**

When to use direct speech

■ Direct speech can be useful in essays to add interest and vividness:

▶ by showing the exact words a person uses, you can build up a clear picture of their character, speech mannerisms and dialect

▶ by using appropriate dialogue for your characters, you can create an authentic atmosphere.

■ Don't over-use direct speech as it slows the story down and can become boring. Use direct speech only if it adds to your story.

■ Direct speech is usually unsuitable for other formal writing tasks. It is generally preferable to summarise comments, opinions or conversation in formal letters and reports, unless the words have a particular significance, and then you can quote them.

Indirect speech

We use indirect speech more frequently than we use direct speech. It is quicker to write in essays because you don't have to worry about the punctuation as you do in direct speech.

Examples: The surveyor said it would be preferable to have a larger dormer window.

My son said that he was sorry he had not phoned me on Sunday.

The examiner said he was pleased to see the candidate had used a wide and varied vocabulary.

In indirect speech you identify the speaker before you describe what he or she said.

Other quotations

When you quote the exact words from other sources, for instance books, plays, poems, newspapers and notices, you enclose the words in quotation marks to show that they aren't your own words.

Examples: D.H. Lawrence described money as, 'Money is our madness, our vast collective madness' in the first line of his poem 'Money-Madness'.

H.G. Wells, in 'The History of Mr Polly', describes Mr Polly's eyes as, 'ruddy brown and troubled, and the left one was round with more wonder in it than its fellow.'

You can also enclose the *titles* of poems, books, plays, newspapers, and radio and television programmes in quotation marks:

I have just been reading 'The Day it Rained Forever' by Ray Bradbury.

However, you may find that in books and other publications italic type is used instead, *without* quotation marks: *The Day it Rained Forever*. Either system is correct, but it will be easier for you to use quotation marks.

Checkpoints

Quotation marks are used to enclose the exact words spoken in dialogue.

Learn how to punctuate dialogue so that you can use it to effect in essays.

Don't over-use direct speech in essays. Only use it if it will add to your essay in some way.

Reported speech doesn't need quotation marks. It summarises what a person has said but doesn't use the exact words spoken.

Quotation marks are used for quotations, and can be used for the titles of books, poems and other publications.

---

12   Semicolons

What are semicolons?

- A semicolon is a punctuation mark consisting of a full stop placed over a comma **;**
- Semicolons are used to indicate a pause in a sentence.

Why are semicolons important?

- They give you greater flexibility in your writing and allow you to consider the effect you want to create.
- They are part of standard English and you are expected to be able to use them correctly in GCSE English exams.

What are semicolons used for?

Semicolons are used for:

- closely related statements
- contrast
- lists.

Semicolons for closely related statements

- A semicolon can be used to separate two closely related, independent statements, for instance:

  There are fourteen girls in this class; last year there were nineteen.

- To use a semicolon in this way, each statement either side of the semicolon must be a sentence in its own right.
- The word after a semicolon doesn't need a capital letter unless there is a specific reason for this. (See Chapter 4 *Capital Letters*.)

You could also have written and punctuated this in these ways:

> There are fourteen girls in this class. Last year there were nineteen.
> *(two separate sentences)*

> There are fourteen girls in this class, whereas last year there were nineteen.
> (*one sentence joined by the conjunction* **whereas**)

Each version is correct but creates a slightly different effect.

- A *semicolon* indicates a shorter pause than a full stop, so allowing you to see the close relationship between the two parts.
- A *full stop* indicates the separate nature of the two sentences.
- A *comma* before a *conjunction* linking two sentences together allows for an even shorter pause. The effect of using a comma is less dramatic than using either a semicolon or full stop.

Semicolons for contrast

- A semicolon can be used to join two sentences which indicate a sharp contrast.

Examples: Neil listens to classical music; his son prefers traditional jazz.
I find French and German easy; physics is a nightmare.
Jade is dark, vivacious and very pretty; her younger sister is blonde, shy and rather plain.

Semicolons for lists

In Chapter 8 *Commas* you are advised to use commas for lists.

- You can also use semicolons for lists. They are sometimes preferable in a long, complicated list that already contains commas.

Examples: The sports complex has excellent facilities: a swimming pool with a flume; a jacuzzi which holds at least ten people; a multigym with the latest high-tech equipment; an indoor five-a-side pitch.

Sam had numerous adventurous ideas for his stag night: white water rafting, but this depended on there being enough water in the stream; racing at Silverstone, if Graham could get them tickets; a trip in a hot-air balloon, evening or morning only; or a day's pony trekking in Wales.

If commas had been used to separate the items in these lists, the effect would have been confusing. Semicolons make the divisions clearer.

Checkpoints

■ Semicolons can be used:
  ▶ for closely related statements
  ▶ for contrasting statements
  ▶ in long or complicated lists.
■ A semicolon is followed by a lower-case letter (unless there is a specific reason for using a capital letter).
■ Remember, different punctuation marks create different effects.

13   Colons

What are colons?
- A colon is a punctuation mark formed by two full stops, one written above the other :

Why are colons important?
- There are specific reasons for using colons in writing. These reasons are quite clear.
- They are part of standard English and you are expected to be able to use them correctly in GCSE English exams.

What are colons used for?
Colons are used to:
- introduce lists
- introduce speech and quotations
- explain, expand or summarise.

Colons to introduce lists
- This is the most common use for the colon. It makes the reader pause and it indicates that a list follows.

  Example: When I start decorating my flat, I shall need several things: a step ladder, scissors, a wallpaper brush, a paste table, a range of paintbrushes, and a roller for emulsion.

- You don't need to put a dash after a colon: the colon is sufficient on its own.
- You only need a capital letter after a colon at the beginning of a list for a specific purpose.

  Example: I've seen several films recently: 'When We Were Kings', 'Anna Karenina', 'Everyone Says I Love You' and 'Fever Pitch'.

Colons to introduce speech and quotations

▦ A colon can be used to introduce a passage of direct speech or a quotation, but it is more usual to use a comma.

Examples: Terry insisted: 'We must forget the past and move forward in a new and more positive direction.'

In your previous essay you stated: 'Gladstone was less effective in Ireland than Disraeli.'

Colons to explain, expand or summarise

▦ A colon is used to divide one part of a sentence from another when the second half:

▷ explains

▷ expands

▷ or summarises the first half.

Examples: I feel so happy: I have passed my driving test.

Myra was determined: she would go to university.

An example of his unreliability was seen last week: his absence from the play rehearsal.

In each of these examples a colon is used to show that something will follow: an explanation, an expansion of the first point, or a summary.

▦ You can test that you are using a colon correctly if you think of a colon standing for the word **'namely'**. Test this out in the three examples above.

It doesn't work in the following example:

I sat down to eat my tea: the phone rang. ✗

The two sentences aren't connected and the 'namely' test doesn't work. The second half – **the phone rang** – doesn't explain, expand or summarise the first half.

Checkpoints

▦ Colons can be used for:

▷ introducing lists

▷ introducing a passage of dialogue or a quotation

▷ dividing one part of a sentence from another when the second part explains, expands or summarises the first part.

▦ A colon is followed by a lower-case letter (unless there is a specific reason for using a capital letter).

▦ Learn the reasons for using colons and then you will be able to use them correctly in your writing.

SECTION 2
grammar

14 Introducing Grammar

What is grammar?
- Grammar is the system of rules which covers:
  - the way words are used (their function within a sentence)
  - how words are grouped together.
- In any language, words have to be grouped together in an accepted order so that we can understand one another.

Example: He stopped snow the when to intended go out.

We know the meanings of all these words but they do not make sense to us because they are not in an accepted order.

He intended to go out when the snow stopped.

or

When the snow-stopped, he intended to go out.

Each of these groupings makes complete sense and so forms a sentence.

In Chapters 2 and 3, you saw the importance of sentences and basic sentence punctuation. You may like to refresh your memory about these when you have finished this chapter.

Why is grammar important?
- Grammar is one of the writing skills. Good grammar allows you to make your 'message' clear and unambiguous.
- Understanding grammar can make you feel more confident about the writing process.
- It also enables you to speak correctly and exactly when you are in a formal situation.
- If you appreciate and know the grammar of the English language, you will be able to learn the grammar of a foreign language more readily.
- Using correct grammar can gain you marks in GCSE exams, in English and in other subjects, where a percentage of marks is awarded for spelling, punctuation and grammar.

Understanding grammar

▨ Correct grammar is considered to be part of standard English.

▨ Everyone's language is unique, but, as you have seen, it also has to conform to current, acceptable conventions.

▨ You probably use many grammatical convention without being aware of them. (There may be others that you misuse and these will be the ones you will need to learn.)

▨ Words can be divided into categories according to their functions in sentences.

▨ These word categories are often called *parts of speech*:

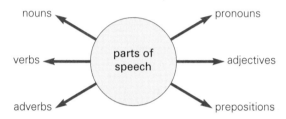

▨ When you look up a word in a good dictionary, you will see that its part of speech (usually as an abbreviation) is given.

handsome, (adj.) good-looking: well-proportioned: dignified: liberal or noble: generous: ample. – (adv.) **handsomely**. – (n) **handsomeness**.

—from *Chambers Concise Dictionary*

▨ Knowing the function of a word in a sentence helps you to use the word correctly.

▨ However, a word can often have one function in one sentence but a different function in another sentence.

Example: His **gamble** was successful.   I never **gamble**
                    /   \
              noun   verb

For you to do
Look back through essays you have written and note down any points about your use of grammar that teachers have suggested you should work on.

Checkpoints

- Grammar is the set of conventions which every language needs if people are to communicate with each other.
- It involves knowing about the function of words in sentences and the order the words are arranged.
- You may already know a great deal about English grammar, because since you were a small child you have been using your knowledge of grammar to form sentences.
- Correct grammar is important – it can help you to gain marks in exams.
- Using correct grammar will help you to express your ideas more clearly and accurately.

15   Nouns

What is a noun?

A noun names a person, place, animal, thing, idea, emotion or quality.

Examples: sister   Carl   Manchester   Sainsbury's   horse   computer   Saturday
vegetarianism   fear   mercy

This chapter tells you how to recognise various types of noun, and how they are used within sentences.

Why is it important to know about nouns?

Being able to recognise nouns helps you to:

- check that you have included a subject in a sentence (see the section **Nouns in sentences** on page 59)
- use capital letters correctly (see the section **Common noun or proper noun?** on page 58 and Chapter 4 *Capital Letters*).

What are the different types of noun?

Knowing that there are various types of noun helps you to identify nouns, but it is more important to recognise nouns than to remember the names of the four categories:

proper nouns

common nouns

abstract nouns

collective nouns

Proper nouns

These are the names of particular:

people	Maxine	Amos	Evita
places	France	Edinburgh	River Plate
buildings	Eiffel Tower	Colosseum	Tate Gallery

months	January	May	September
days	Sunday	Tuesday	Friday
festivals	Eid	Diwali	Easter
companies	Telewest	Lloyds	Asda
organisations	European Union	Oxfam	Greenpeace
animals	Gromit	Tiddles	Lassie
transport	Eurostar	Concorde	HMS Belfast

- As you can see from the examples above, a proper noun always begins with a capital letter.

Common nouns

- These are the general names of people, places, animals or things.

  Examples: students   traffic   college   airport   cats   company

- Most common nouns can be singular or plural.

Common noun or proper noun?

- Some nouns can be either proper nouns or common nouns depending on how they are used in a sentence.

  Example: Their house is near the **River Thames**.

  /

  proper noun – names a particular river

  Their house is by the **river**.

  /

  common noun – does not give the name of a particular river

Abstract nouns

- These nouns name qualities, feeling or ideas.

  Examples: hunger   equality   satisfaction   bitterness   mercy   kindness

Collective nouns

- These name a complete set or group of people, animals or things.

  Examples: an audience   *a group of spectators or listeners*
  a library   *a collection of books*
  a swarm   *a group of insects*

▓ A collective noun usually needs a singular verb.

Example: The audience **was** silent during the final speech.
/
singular verb

There is more about this in Chapter 17 *Verbs*.

Nouns in sentences
Nouns as subjects

▓ Every sentence contains a subject (or implied subject).

▓ The subject of a sentence carries out the action in the sentence. (See Chapter 2 *Sentences* for more about subjects.)

▓ A noun can be the subject of a sentence.

Examples: **Mark** hopes to study art and design at college.
\
subject – a proper noun

Our **society** no longer cares about poverty.
\
subject – a common noun

If you are checking a sentence for a subject, remember the subject can often be a noun but can also be a pronoun. (See Chapter 16 *Pronouns*.)

Nouns as objects

▓ A noun can also be the object of a sentence.

▓ The object is the person, place or thing that an action is carried out upon.

Examples: Manjit drove my **car**.
/
object – a common noun

Snow filled the **ditches** for most of February.
/
object – a common noun

▓ Not every sentence has an object.

a versus *an*

If you are uncertain whether to use **a** or **an** before a noun, use this check.

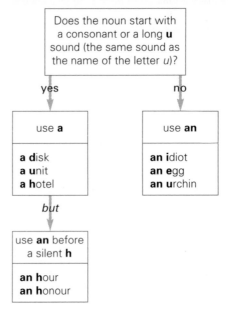

```
         Does the noun start with
         a consonant or a long u
         sound (the same sound as
         the name of the letter u)?

    yes                          no

┌──────────────┐        ┌──────────────┐
│    use a     │        │    use an    │
├──────────────┤        ├──────────────┤
│  a disk      │        │  an idiot    │
│  a unit      │        │  an egg      │
│  a hotel     │        │  an urchin   │
└──────────────┘        └──────────────┘
      but

┌──────────────┐
│ use an before│
│  a silent h  │
├──────────────┤
│  an hour     │
│  an honour   │
└──────────────┘
```

Checkpoints

- Nouns are used to name people, places, animals, things, ideas, emotions or qualities.
- It is not essential to remember all the different types but you will find it helpful to be able to recognise nouns in sentences.
- Proper nouns (names of particular people, places, animals or things) always start with a capital letter. (See Chapter 4 *Capital Letters*.)

16 Pronouns

What is a pronoun?

- A pronoun is a word that is used instead of a noun.

  Examples: him   this   ourselves   theirs   either   who   that

- We use them to refer to a person or thing we have already mentioned by name.

  Example: **Sian** worked hard all evening as **she** wanted to finish the assignment.

We have used the pronoun **she** to replace the noun **Sian**.

Why is it important to know about pronouns?

- As pronouns save us from repeating a noun in a sentence, they make our writing and speech more fluent and natural.

  Example: **Harry** and **Wendy** live in a flat which **Harry** and **Wendy** rent from **Harry** and **Wendy's** friends.

By replacing some of these nouns by pronouns, the sentence is less wordy and repetitive, and more natural:

  Harry and **Wendy** live in a flat which **they** rent from **their** friends.

- If you understand the work that pronouns do in sentences, you can choose the exact pronoun for a given situation.
- You will find it helpful to know about pronouns when you are learning a foreign language.

What are the different types of pronoun?

- You have already seen that there are different types of noun: pronouns can also be divided into categories.
- You do not need to remember the name of each category, but you should understand the work each type does in sentences.

  personal   reflexive   interrogative

  possessive   relative   demonstrative

  others

▓ Don't be daunted by this list. Read through this chapter slowly and then return to any that you need to study in more detail.

Personal pronouns
▓ This is probably the easiest category to recognise.
▓ It contains:

I   he   she   we   they   you   it   me   him   her   us   them

Examples: **They** won a glorious victory.
           We spent two weeks on work experience.
           You must be careful.

▓ In each of the sentences above the personal pronoun is the *subject* of the sentence. (Look back at the section **Nouns as subjects** in Chapter 15 *Nouns* if you are uncertain about this.)
▓ In each of the sentences below the personal pronoun is the *object* of the sentence.

Examples: A policeman approached **them**.
           Jacob came to **us** last week.
           Shusma will help **you**.

▓ You will notice that in some instances the personal pronoun changes when it is used as the object of a sentence.
  ▸ **You** and **it** remain the same regardless of whether they are used as the subject or object of a sentence.
  ▸ The other personal pronouns change according to whether they are the subject or object of a sentence.

Personal pronouns with prepositions
▓ The object form of each personal pronoun is also used when a personal pronoun follows a preposition. (If you need to check what a preposition is, turn to Chapter 20.)

Examples: I received a letter **from him**.
                              /   \
                     preposition   object form of personal pronoun

           Do not hold it **against me**.
                           /   \
                  preposition   object form of pronoun

Common mistakes

▓ Using a personal pronoun in a sentence can sometimes confuse your reader.

Example: The doctor told her patient **she** was suffering from 'flu.
                                                /
                        *Does **she** refer to the doctor or the patient?*

▓ You have seen that the object form of the personal pronoun is **me**, but sometimes **I** (the subject form) is used by mistake.

Examples: Tina will meet Tony and **I** outside the cinema. ✗
                 Tina will meet Tony and **me** outside the cinema. ✓

                 He stood next to Martin and **I** in the queue. ✗
                 He stood next to Martin and **me** in the queue. ✓

▓ If you are uncertain whether to use **I** or **me** in such instances, check by removing the other person's name:

                 He stood next to **me** in the queue. ✓

You can see immediately that **I** is wrong and **me** is correct.

Possessive pronouns

▓ These are used to show ownership:

mine   yours   his   hers   ours   theirs

Examples: That book is **hers**.
                 If that cat is **yours**, where is **ours**?

Common mistake

▓ Some students try to put an apostrophe with a possessive pronoun. This is incorrect.

▓ A noun needs an apostrophe to show ownership, but a possessive pronoun does not. (See Chapter 10 *Apostrophes*.)

Example: **Jean's** car goes faster than **yours**.
                        /   \
                 noun has an apostrophe   possessive pronoun has no apostrophe

Reflexive pronouns

myself   yourself   himself   herself   itself
ourselves   yourselves   themselves

- A reflexive pronoun *refers* (reflects back) to the subject of the sentence.

Example: **Kevin** prepared **himself** for the fight.

  /   \

  subject   *reflexive pronoun (refers **to Kevin**)*

- It must be the correct reflexive pronoun to use with the subject.

Example: **She** blamed **herself** for their problems.
  *(The subject is **she** so the reflexive pronoun is **herself**.)*

Relative pronouns

who   whom   whose   which   that

- A relative pronoun is used to replace a noun or pronoun that has already been used earlier in the sentence.
- A relative pronoun also acts like a *conjunction*, and joins sentences, or main and subordinate clauses, together to make one sentence. (See Chapter 3 *More Sentences*.)

Examples: There is Laura. She is a set designer for 'Brookside'.
  There is Laura, **who** is a set designer for 'Brookside'.
  (***Who** replaces **she** and joins the two sentences.)*

  I like your trainers. You bought the trainers last week.
  I like the trainers **which** you bought last week.
  (***Which** replaces the noun **trainers** and joins the two sentences.)*

- In the second example above the relative pronoun could be omitted. This often happens in English and is quite correct.

Examples: I like the trainers you bought last week. (***which** is omitted)*
  The library has a copy of the book **that** Susan wanted. (***that** could be left out of the sentence)*

Whom
- **Whom** is the object form of **who**.
- It is used to refer to the object of a verb.

Example: Bill spoke to the girl. He had met **her** at a party.

  /

  *object of the verb **had met***

Bill spoke to the girl **whom** he had met at a party.
/
relative pronoun in the object form

- Although **whom** is the correct form for writing, we often use **who** in speech.
- **Whom** is used after a preposition. (For more about prepositions, see Chapter 20 *Prepositions*.)

Example: The man **with whom** I was travelling has just written his first novel.

In speech and formal writing, we are more likely to express this as:
The man **who** I was travelling **with** has just written his first novel.
or The man I was travelling **with** has just written his first novel. (***who** is omitted*)

Interrogative pronouns
who   whom   whose   which   what
- Interrogative pronouns are used to ask questions.

Examples: **Who** is shouting?
To **whom** is Stephen talking?
Whose is that?
Which would you prefer?
What will be the effect of global warming?

Demonstrative pronouns
this   that   these   those
- Demonstrative pronouns replace nouns, and point out or demonstrate a particular person or thing.

Examples: Dave worked on **this** for six hours.
That is my idea of a hero.
I think **these** are better than **those**.

Other pronouns

some	someone	somebody	something
any	anyone	anybody	anything
	everyone	everybody	everything
few	many	more	most
no-one	nobody	nothing	
none	either	neither	each

▨ All of the words in the box on page 65 can be pronouns when they are used to replace a noun.

Examples: **Nobody** was aware of the outcome.
I know he has **some**.

Common mistakes
▨ The pronouns in italic type in the box on page 65 take a singular verb. (See also Chapter 17 *Verbs*.) People sometimes forget to use the singular verb with these pronouns.

Examples: During the war everyone **was** asked to contribute.
/   \
pronoun   *singular verb*

Something **is** wrong.
/   \
pronoun   *singular verb*

▨ Remember, all the pronouns that need a singular verb also need singular personal pronouns.

Examples: Everyone must do **his** best all the time.

To avoid only using a 'masculine' pronoun, this is sometimes written as:
Everyone must do **his/her** best all the time.

In speech we often use a plural pronoun:
Everyone must do **their** best all the time.

Checkpoints

▨ Pronouns are used to replace nouns.

▨ Using pronouns helps you to write clear and precise English.

▨ When you proof-read your writing, look for sentences that would be more fluent if you replaced a noun with a pronoun.

▨ You can sometimes avoid writing a series of short, jerky sentences by using relative pronouns to join sentences together.

▨ There is a great deal to learn about pronouns. Use this chapter as a reference source when you need to 'brush up' your knowledge of pronouns, particularly when you are studying a foreign language.

▨ Some pronouns do not belong to only one category of pronoun. The category depends on the role the pronoun performs in a sentence.

▨ Remember, some of the pronouns shown in this chapter can also be other parts of speech, depending on their function in a sentence. You will notice this when you work through Chapter 18 *Adjectives*.

17 | Verbs

What is a verb?

▪ A verb is a word that expresses an action.

> Examples: Lucy **kicked** the ball.   He **is writing** a letter.
>
> /   \
>
> verb   verb

▪ A verb can also show a state of being.

> Example: She **is** fourteen.   I **am** unhappy.
>
> /   \
>
> verb   verb

▪ Sometimes a verb needs one or more words to complete it. These additional words are called auxiliary verbs.

> Examples: I **am going** to Birmingham
>
> /   \
>
> auxiliary   main
> verb   verb
>
> Sharon **had spoken**.
>
> /   \
>
> auxiliary verb   main verb

▪ Auxiliary verbs support the main verb in a sentence.
▪ They help to form the tense of the main verb. (See the section **Verb tenses** on page 71.)

> Example: Steve **was finishing** his homework.
>
> /   \
>
> auxiliary verb helps to form past tense of main verb

▪ Auxiliary verbs can also help to form questions.

> Example: **Do** you **like** coffee?
>
> | \
>
> auxiliary   main
> verb   verb

Why is it important to know about verbs?

- Verbs play an essential part in sentence construction. In Chapter 2 *Sentences* you saw that every sentence must contain a verb. (See also the section **Verbs in sentences** below.)

- By being able to recognise verbs, you can check for a verb if you are uncertain whether you have written a sentence.

- You can avoid many common errors. You will find out about these as you work through this chapter.

- You need to understand verbs and tenses (see pages 71–72) when you learn a foreign language.

Verbs in sentences

- As you saw in Chapter 2, a sentence is made up of two parts:
  - a *subject* (who or what the sentence is about)
  - a *predicate* (which tells us more about the subject).
- A verb is the most important part of the predicate.
- A predicate must contain a verb.

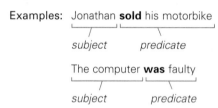

Examples: Jonathan **sold** his motorbike

          subject   *predicate*

        The computer **was** faulty

          subject   *predicate*

Agreement of verbs and subjects

- Verb forms can differ according to who is carrying out the action.
- These are the forms, in the present tense, of the verb **to walk**.

	singular	plural
first person	I walk	we walk
second person	you walk	you walk
third person	he/she/it walks	they walk

▓ The verb in the predicate of a sentence must have the correct form for its subject. This is called *agreement* between the verb and its subject.

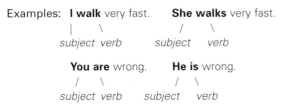

Examples: **I walk** very fast.   **She walks** very fast.

| \
subject verb   subject   verb

You are wrong.   **He is** wrong.

/ \   / \
subject verb   subject   verb

▓ If you wrote:

I walks very fast. ✗
He are wrong. ✗

you would have chosen the wrong form of verb for the subject and your sentence would be ungrammatical.

▓ If English is your first language, in most instances you will automatically choose the right form of the verb for the subject.

▓ When you are learning a foreign language it may take you a considerable amount of practice to make the correct choice every time.

▓ People often have difficulties choosing the correct form of verb to agree with the subject in these instances:

▶ double subjects

▶ singular subjects appearing to be plural

▶ collective nouns.

Double subjects

▓ Where the subject of a sentence is made up of two or more separate subjects, the verb is generally used in the plural form.

The **manager** and his **secretary were** both at the meeting.

\   /   \
double subject   third person plural verb

The **weather**, the **pitch** and the **lack of support were** all to blame.

\ | /   \
three subjects   third person plural verb

Singular subjects appearing to be plural

▨ Some common nouns ending in s appear to be plural but are singular, so need the singular form of the verb.

Examples: **Mathematics is** the Queen of the Sciences.
/ \
singular subject   third person singular verb

The **news was** frightening.
/ \
singular subject   third person singular verb

▨ Here are some other singular words which can also cause confusion. They are all used with a singular verb.

anybody	everyone	nothing
everybody	no-one	something
nobody	someone	each
somebody	either	everything
anyone	anything	neither

Examples: Everybody **likes** Geoff.
Is anyone there?
Everyone **wants** them to win.

▨ You may sometimes be uncertain which form of a verb to use because the word placed immediately before the verb appears to indicate a plural subject.

Examples: **Each** of the girls **has** to wait for an answer
| \
subject   singular verb

The **box** of books **was** damaged.
/ \
subject   singular verb

Collective nouns

▨ As you saw in Chapter 15, a collective noun is generally considered to be a single unit and so has a singular verb form.

Example: The council **is** trying to save money.

Although the council comprises several people, it is judged to be a single unit in this instance.

■ If the separate parts of the unit are being emphasised in the sentence, then a plural form of the verb is required.

Example: My family **have** different views on politics.

We are stressing that the family is not a single unit but several separate people, each with a different view, so we need the plural form of the verb.

For you to do
To help you recall the points we have covered about the agreement of verbs and subjects, try choosing the correct form of the verb in each of these sentences.

Either he **leave/leaves** or I do.
A house and a bungalow in my street **has/have** been burnt down.
Only one of her children **has/have** visited her.
Neither of the two boys **were/was** guilty.
The whole factory **is/are** closing for a week in June.
Everyone in the room **is/are** busy.

Verb tenses
■ The verb form shows the time when an action takes place.
■ The verb form may be in the *present, past* or *future* tense.

Examples: It **is** snowing. (*present tense*)
Leroy **bought** some inline skates. (*past tense*)
Helen **will be coming** to the meeting. (*future*)

■ Most verbs follow a pattern in forming each of the tenses and are referred to as *regular verbs*.
■ *Irregular verbs* form the tenses in a variety of different ways.

Present tense
There are two main ways of showing this:

present simple tense   I **eat**.
present continuous tense   I **am eating**.

Past tense
This can be shown in various ways:

past simple tense	She **watched** the television.
past continuous tense	She **was watching** the television.
perfect tense	She **has watched** the television.
pluperfect tense	She **had watched** the television.

(The pluperfect tense is further back in time than the perfect tense.)

Future tense
There are several ways of expressing future time, but in general we use **shall** or **will** as the auxiliary verb, together with a main verb:

I **shall see** you later.
The school **will close** on Friday.

In informal writing, we often use the **going to** construction:

We **are going to watch** Manchester United on Saturday.

Common mistakes
▓ Sometimes when you are writing, it is easy to drift unintentionally from one tense to another.

Example: I **opened** the door and he **jumps** out at me. ✗
              /   \
          past tense   *present tense*

▓ You must be aware of tense when you are writing and correcting a first draft.

▓ If you are writing a narrative or descriptive English essay, it is generally easier to write in the past tense.

▓ You may find that occasionally you write in the present tense to create the right effect, but it can be difficult to sustain.

Active and passive verbs
▓ When the subject of a clause or sentence carries out an action, the verb is *active*.

Example: **Peter kicked** the ball away from the goal area.
             | \
          subject   *active verb*

When the subject has the action done to it, the verb is *passive*.

Example: **The ball was kicked** away from the goal area.

subject   passive verb

Normally you should use active verbs in your writing as they create a more direct and less wordy style.

Checkpoints

It is important to recognise and understand the function of verbs.

Every sentence must contain a verb.

When you read through a first draft of your writing, pay particular attention to the common mistakes we have outlined in this chapter.

As this chapter contains a number of points, you may decide to go back through it a number of times to make sure you have a full understanding of the function of verbs.

---

18 Adjectives

What is an adjective?

▨ An adjective gives more information (usually descriptive information) about a noun or pronoun.

The **thin boy** held a **torn, yellow flag** in his **right hand**
   /   \   /   \   /   \
adjective noun   adjectives   noun adjective noun

Six people ran from the **ruined building**.
  | \   /   \
adjective noun   adjective   noun

He is **ugly**.
  | \
pronoun adjective

▨ Adjectives usually go before the word they describe, but they can be placed elsewhere in the sentence (as in the last example above).

This tomato is **soft** and **mouldy**.
  | \ | \
adjective noun adjective adjective

My suitcase is **heavy**.
  | \   \
adjective noun   adjective

▨ You will have noticed that you can use more than one adjective to add description to a noun or pronoun.

A **tantalising, aromatic, spicy smell** wafted across the room.
        /   \
adjectives   noun

It is always **noisy, smoky** and **dark**.
  | /
pronoun   adjectives

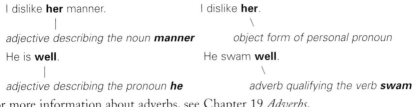

■ Some adjectives can cause confusion because the same words can have different functions in other sentences.

I dislike **her** manner.   I dislike **her**.

adjective describing the noun ***manner***   *object form of personal pronoun*

He is **well**.   He swam **well**.

adjective describing the pronoun ***he***   *adverb qualifying the verb* ***swam***

For more information about adverbs, see Chapter 19 *Adverbs*.

Why is it important to know about adjectives?

■ By choosing suitable adjectives and using them carefully, you can make your writing more interesting and vivid.

■ Adjectives can help you to create a more accurate and realistic 'picture' for your audience. Compare these two passages about an outing to a museum. Which is more interesting and informative?

> On Sunday we went on an outing to Ironbridge. There are several museums and we decided to visit Blists Hill Museum. This museum allows visitors to see what life was like in late Victorian England.

> On Sunday we went on a fascinating day's outing to Ironbridge. There are several industrial museums and we decided to visit the fifty-acre Blists Hill Museum. This spectacular open-air museum allows visitors to see what everyday life was like in late Victorian England.

Choosing adjectives

■ A thesaurus will provide you with a range of alternative adjectives.

■ A dictionary can help you choose the most appropriate adjectives from the range.

■ Avoid adjectives that are used so frequently that have become almost meaningless, for instance **big, nice** or **lovely**.

■ Remember, don't use too many adjectives in your writing: aim for quality, not quantity.

■ The Vocabulary section in GCSE *English Spelling and Vocabulary* also provides advice on using descriptive words to improve your writing.

For you to do

Use a thesaurus and a dictionary to find suitable adjectives to add detail and description to the nouns in the following sentences. (The nouns are in bold type.)

The **house** had been neglected for thirty years.

The **boy** sat crying in the **road**.

The **town centre** was full of **people**.

The **bird** flew high into the air.

The **door** swung open invitingly.

Choosing adjectives

■ When an adjective is formed from a proper noun, it normally starts with a capital letter. (See also Chapter 4 *Capital Letters*.)

Examples: | **proper noun** | **adjective** |
| --- | --- |
| China | Chinese |
| Buddha | Buddhist |
| Victoria | Victorian |

The **French** trawler drifted into the harbour.
He was the most famous **Shakespearean** actor of his time.

What do adjectives do?

Adjectives:

add description

show ownership

question

identify

indicate quantity

Add description

- As you have already seen in previous examples, most adjectives add description to a noun or pronoun.

Examples: a **marvellous idea**   a **soft, balmy evening**

- This type of adjective is easy to recognise. Other types of adjectives can be more difficult to identify.

Show ownership

my   you   his   her   its   our   their

- There are all *possessive adjectives* when they show who the owner is.

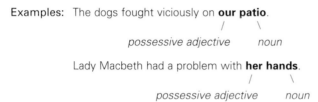

Examples: The dogs fought viciously on **our patio**.

possessive adjective   noun

Lady Macbeth had a problem with **her hands**.

possessive adjective   noun

His can also be a possessive pronoun, and **her** is also the object form of the personal pronoun **she**. See Chapter 16 *Pronouns*, pages 62 and 63. It depends upon their use within a sentence.

Question

which   what

These words can be used as questioning or *interrogative adjectives* when they accompany a noun.

Examples: **Which department** is he in?
What size is that?

- You have already seen in Chapter 16 *Pronouns*, page 65, that **which** and **what** can also function as *interrogative pronouns* when they replace a noun.

Identify

this   that   these   those

- When these words are linked to a noun they are *demonstrative adjectives* – they identify the noun.

Examples: **Those children** are working well together.
That jet ski is too near to the beach.

■ When **this, that, these** and **those** are used to replace a noun, they are *demonstrative pronouns*. See Chapter 16 *Pronouns*, page 65.

Indicate quantity

■ Adjectives can show the exact quantity of the accompanying noun.

Examples: The moon was in its **first phase**.
Twelve students will be going on the French exchange trip.

■ Adjectives can also show an imprecise amount.

Examples: There were **several people** in the room.
I am sure I have made **more mistakes** this time.
Many accidents are caused through negligence.

Other adjectives

each   every   either   neither

■ These can all be adjectives when they are used to give more information about nouns.

Examples: **Either** book will help you.
The governors studied **every** possibility.

■ **Either** and **neither** can also be used as pronouns. See Chapter 16 *Pronouns*, page 65.

■ Remember, **each, every, either** and **neither** are followed by a singular verb (see Chapter 17 *Verbs*, page 70) unless two different plural groups of people or things are referred to.

Examples: **Every** pupil **is** expected to attend.
            \
            singular verb

Neither cars **nor** lorries are allowed into the town during the fair.
            \   \
*two groups – **cars***   *plural verb*
*and **lorries***

■ **Either** and **or** go together, and **neither** is followed by **nor**. People sometimes confuse these pairs.

Examples: I'd like to visit **either** Spain **or** Portugal this summer.
Neither Joseph **nor** Danny was interviewed.

Using adjectives for comparison

Examples: Folkestone to Boulogne is a **short** route across the Channel.
Portsmouth to Le Havre is a **shorter** route than Plymouth to Roscoff.
Dover to Calais is the **shortest** route across the Channel.

- In the first example above, we are making a *positive* statement about the route: we are describing it as a **short** route. No comparison is taking place.
- In the second sentence **shorter** is used to compare *two* routes. We use the *comparative* form of the adjective.
- In the third sentence we are comparing *more than two* routes, so we use **shortest**, the *superlative* form.

Single-syllable adjectives

- When you want to use the *comparative* or *superlative* forms of a single-syllable adjective, add -**er** or -**est**.

Examples: | **positive** | **comparative** | **superlative** |
|---|---|---|
| bright | brighter | brightest |
| tall | taller | tallest |

Two or more syllables

- When an adjective has two or more syllables, we usually add **more** or **most** in front of the adjective to make the comparative/superlative forms.

Examples: | **positive** | **comparative** | **superlative** |
|---|---|---|
| dramatic *(3 syllables)* | more dramatic | most dramatic |
| intelligent *(4 syllables)* | more intelligent | most intelligent |

This room is **more comfortable** than the last one.
He is the **most cautious** man I have ever known.

- Some words which end in **y** do not follow the guidelines.

Example: **lucky** has two syllables (luc / ky)
I am **luckier** this year than last. (not **more lucky**)

▦ Certain common adjectives do not obey the guidelines either. Their comparative and superlative forms are totally irregular.

Examples: positive	comparative	superlative
good	better	best
bad	worse	worst
much	more	most
many	more	most
little	less	least

I have **good** eyesight.
Alex's eyesight is **better** than mine.
Clare has the **best** eyesight.

Common mistakes

▦ People sometimes choose the wrong form of comparison.

Example: His writing is **worst** than mine. ✗
His writing is **worse** than mine. ✓

▦ Some adjectives have no comparative or superlative forms.

Example: This is the **most unique** building. ✗

This is impossible as **unique** means the only one of its kind – it cannot be compared with others.

This is a **unique** building. ✓

Checkpoints

▦ Adjectives add description or detail to nouns and pronouns.
▦ If you choose and use them wisely, they will improve your writing and speech by making them more precise or vivid.
▦ Follow our advice for avoiding common mistakes with adjectives.

19 Adverbs

What is an adverb?

▧ An adverb usually gives more information about a verb.

Examples: The cat **stretched sleepily**.
　　　　　　　　　／　　　　＼
　　　　　　　verb　　　adverb (tells us **how** the cat stretched)

The parcel **arrived yesterday**.
　　　　　　／　　　＼
　　　　verb　　　adverb (tells us **when** the parcel arrived)

▧ An adverb can give more information about an adjective.

Example: Simon was **very tall** for his age.
　　　　　　　　　／　＼
　　　　　　　adverb　　adjective
　　　　　(tells us **how tall**)

▧ An adverb can also give more information about another adverb.

Example: I wrote my essay **quite quickly**.
　　　　　　　　　　　／　　　＼
　　　adverb (modifies **quickly**)　adverb (tells **how** it was written)

▧ When an adverb gives more information about a verb, adjective or adverb, it is said to *modify* that word.

▧ As you can see from the examples above, many adverbs end in -**ly** and are formed from an adjective. These adverbs are easy to recognise.

Examples: **adjective**　　**adverb**
　　　　　foolish　　　foolishly
　　　　　heavy　　　　heavily
　　　　　thoughtful　　thoughtfully

▧ Adverbs which do not end in -**ly** include:

twice	so	about
enough	far	almost
perhaps	rather	well

▓ Remember, a word may function as several different parts of speech. Look at how the word is being used in a sentence to decide which part of speech it is.

Examples: He drove the **fast** car with skill and determination.

|

adjective describing the noun ***car***

He walked **fast**.

|

adverb showing how ***he walked****.*

Why is it important to know about adverbs?

▓ In Chapter 18 *Adjectives*, you saw that by using descriptive words you can create a vivid and exact 'picture'.

▓ Adverbs can also add colour and precision to your speech and writing.

Example: Tim spoke **enthusiastically** and **knowledgeably** about his holiday in Africa.

This sentence has less impact if the adverbs **enthusiastically** and **knowledgeably** are removed:

Tim spoke about his holiday in Africa.

▓ If too many adverbs are used in a piece of writing, it can become tedious and contrived.

Example: 'Where have you been?' demanded Julian angrily.
'Nowhere', she replied defensively.
He strode purposefully towards her. Louise edged timidly back until, reaching nervously for the door, she ran swiftly from the room.

▓ You should also take care to choose appropriate adverbs for the situation.

For you to do

Using a thesaurus and dictionary, choose suitable adverbs for each of these verbs:

talked   fought   argued   think   slept   played   ran   drank

Adverbs in sentences
▓ There are no rules to tell you where to place an adverb in a sentence.
▓ An adverb is usually placed near the verb, adjective or adverb it modifies. However, this depends upon the type of adverb and the stress placed upon it.
▓ If you are in doubt, use your knowledge of what sounds right.

For example, where do you think the adverb **slowly** should be placed in this sentence?

He crawled towards the door.

Any of these positions is correct:

Slowly he crawled towards the door.

He **slowly** crawled towards the door.

He crawled **slowly** towards the door.

He crawled towards the door **slowly**.

▓ In many foreign languages there are clear guidelines about where to place an adverb. You should follow these guidelines.

What are the different types of adverb?
▓ Types:

adverbs of manner

adverbs of time

adverbs of place

adverbs of degree

interrogative adverbs

sentence adverbs

Adverbs of manner
▓ These provide information about *how* an action is carried out.

Examples: She thanked me **eagerly**.
She thanked me **reluctantly**.
She thanked me **hesitantly**.

Adverbs of time

- These adverbs show *when* an action is carried out.

Examples: The game will be over **soon**.
The game will be over **eventually**.

- They can also show *how often* an action is carried out or *for how long* it continues.

Examples: Imran practises **daily**.
Jacqueline visited London **briefly** while she was in England.

Adverbs of place

- These adverbs tell us *where* an action is carried out.
- These are usually placed next to the verb they modify.

Examples: Come **here**.
The children rushed **in**.

Adverbs of degree

- These can be used to modify verbs, adjectives and other adverbs.
- They give *emphasis to* or *limit* the word they modify.

Examples: This is **so** difficult.
This is **extremely** difficult.
This is **fairly** difficult.

Interrogative adverbs

how   where   when   why

- These are interrogative adverbs and ask about the *manner, time, place* or *reason* for actions.

Examples: **How** did you injure yourself?
Where did you injure yourself?
When did you injure yourself?
Why did you injure yourself?

- **Where, when, how** and **why** are not always used to ask questions: they can also be used to join clauses together in a sentence.

Examples: I am not sure **why** he is unhappy.
They will be here **when** they are ready.

Sentence adverbs

▪ These are used to *express an opinion* or *introduce an idea.*
▪ They are often placed at the beginning of a sentence.
▪ They may be followed by a comma so that the reader pauses and emphasises the opening word of the sentence.

Examples: **Sadly**, our school must close down in July.
Perhaps he was wrong.

Using adverbs for comparison

▪ Adverbs, like adjectives, can be used in comparisons and have similar rules for forming the comparative and superlative.

Examples: I worked **hard** on Sunday. *(**hard** is a single-syllable word)*
I worked **harder** on Monday. *(add **-er** for the comparative form)*
I worked **hardest** on Wednesday. *(add **-est** to form the superlative)*

Sandy spoke **simply**. *(**simply** has two syllables)*
Sandy spoke **more simply** than Simon. *(add **more** to form the comparative)*
Sandy spoke the **most simply** of all the speakers. *(add **most** for the superlative)*

▪ Some adverbs form the comparative and superlative in irregular ways.

Examples: (The adjective form is shown in brackets.)

adverb	comparative	superlative
well (good)	better (better)	best (best)
badly (bad)	worse (worse)	worst (worst)
much (much)	more (more)	most (most)
little (little)	less (less)	least (least)

Common mistake

▪ The comparative and superlative forms are the same for both adverbs and adjectives, but mistakes are sometimes made when **good** and **well, bad** and **badly** are confused.

Example: Sara tackled **good**. ✗

Good is an adjective – what is needed is an adverb to give more information about the verb **tackled**:

Sara tackled **well**. ✓

▓ There are other instances where an adjective is used wrongly in place of an adverb.

Example: Frank fought **strong** throughout the match. ✗
Frank fought **strongly** throughout the match. ✓

▓ If you are uncertain whether an adverb or an adjective is needed, think about the functions of adverbs and adjectives to decide which part of speech is required. (Are you giving more information about a *verb*, *adjective* or *adverb*, or are you describing a *noun* or *pronoun*?)

Checkpoints

▓ Choose suitable adverbs to enhance your writing.

▓ There are no firm rules for where an adverb is placed in a sentence, but it is usually positioned near to the word it modifies.

▓ If you understand the various functions of adverbs, you can check that you are using them correctly.

---

20 Prepositions

What is a preposition?

- The word *preposition* means 'placed before'.
- A preposition usually introduces a phrase containing a noun or pronoun.

Examples: He waited **for hours**.

  / \

  preposition *noun*

  Jenny reached **towards it**.

  / \

  preposition *pronoun*

- A preposition shows the relationship between the noun or pronoun it introduces and another word in the sentence. This relationship usually indicates time or place.

Examples:

time	**place**
We will meet **at** four o'clock.	He rushed **through** the door.
I've been dieting **since** Christmas.	The cellar was **below** the stairs.
They decided to go **on** Sunday.	The cinema is **past** the shops.

- Two or three words are sometimes used together to function as a preposition.

Examples: She walked **away from** the fire.

  The paper is **next to** the typewriter.

  Paul placed the card **in front of** the picture.

- Sometimes a word may be used as a preposition in one sentence but an as adverb in another sentence.

Examples: The chocolate was still **inside** the box.

  /

  preposition

  He ran **inside**.

  /

  adverb giving more information about the verb ***ran***

Why is it important to know about prepositions?

If you are able to recognise prepositions and know how to use them, you may avoid two common errors regarding the use of prepositions:

- using the wrong preposition
- not using the object form of a personal pronoun when it follows a preposition.

(See **Common mistakes** below for help with these points.)

When you learn a foreign language, you will probably need to study the use of prepositions carefully, as selecting the right preposition can sometimes be difficult.

Common mistakes

Correct choice

Unfortunately there isn't a set of guidelines to help us choose the correct preposition for each occasion.

We learn the correct usage by reading, listening and practising.

Examples: I'm bored **of** writing essays. ✗
I'm bored **with** writing essays. ✓

Emma was embarrassed **with** her family. ✗
Emma was embarrassed **by** her family. ✓

This game is very different **to** last week's. ✗
This game is very different **from** last week's. ✓

As you may be aware, grammatical points do change over a period of time, and **different to** is increasingly acceptable in speech.

Pronouns after prepositions

In Chapter 16 *Pronouns*, you saw that the object form of the personal pronoun (**me, you, him, her, it, us, them**) is used when it follows a preposition.

Example: He gave it to **me**. ✓
He gave it to **I**. ✗

Where two different personal pronouns follow a preposition, both are used in the object form.

Example: Peter wrote to **her** and **me**.

Checkpoints

- A preposition is used in a sentence to show a relationship.
- Some words may be prepositions or adverbs according to how they are used in sentences.
- When you proof-read your writing, make sure you have always chosen the correct preposition and, where appropriate, the correct form of personal pronoun.

Glossary

Abbreviation	A shortened word or phrase, often containing full stops.
Adjective	A word that describes or gives more information about a *noun* or *pronoun*.
Demonstrative adjective	Identifies a particular person or object, e.g. **this, that, these, those**.
Interrogative adjective	Accompanies a noun and introduces a question, e.g. **which, what**.
Possessive adjective	Describes a *noun*, indicating who the owner is, e.g. **my, your, his, her, its, our, their**.
Adverb	A word that usually gives more information about a *verb*, explaining *when, how* or *where* an action takes place. It can also give additional information about an *adjective* or another *adverb*.
Adverb of degree	Emphasises or limits the word it modifies.
Adverb of manner	Provides information about how an action is carried out.
Adverb of place	Shows *where* an action happens.
Adverb of time	Shows *when* an action happens.
Interrogative adverb	Asks about the *manner, place, time* or *reason* for an action, e.g. **how, where, when, why**.
Sentence adverb	Introduces an idea or expresses an opinion.
Comparative	The form of an *adjective* or *adverb* that is used to compare two nouns or verbs, e.g. **taller, more useful, more slowly**.
Conjunction	A 'linking' word, used to join two sentences.
Contraction	A shortened word or group of words used in speech, with an apostrophe indicating the missing letters. Contractions are not normally used in formal writing.
Direct question	A question that expects an answer.
Direct speech	The exact words a speaker says.
Indirect speech	Conveys dialogue *without* quoting the exact words.
Main clause	The main statement of a sentence, which makes sense on its own. Also called an *independent clause*.
Noun	A word used to name a *person, place, animal, thing, emotion, feeling* or *idea*.
Abstract noun	Names a *quality, feeling* or *idea* – something intangible.

Collective noun	Names a complete set or group.
Common noun	The general name for a *person, place, animal* or *thing.*
Proper noun	Names a particular *person, place, company, animal,* etc.
Predicate	The predicate gives information about the *subject* of a sentence. It always contains a *verb.*
Preposition	Introduces a phrase containing a *noun* or *pronoun* and shows the relationship between it and another word in the sentence. This relationship usually indicates *time* or *place.*
Pronoun	A word used instead of a *noun.* It refers to a thing or person previously mentioned.
Demonstrative pronoun	Points out a particular person or object. Examples: **this, that, these, those.**
Interrogative pronoun	Replaces a noun and introduces a question. Examples: **who, whom, whose, which, what.**
Personal pronoun	The pronouns **I, you, he, she, it, we** and **they,** and their object forms **me, you, him, her, it, us** and **them.**
Possessive pronoun	The pronoun forms of *possessive adjectives:* **mine, yours, his, hers, ours, theirs.**
Reflexive pronoun	Refers to pronouns used as the subject of the sentence: **myself, yourself, himself, herself, itself, ourselves, yourselves, themselves.**
Relative pronoun	Refers to a noun or pronoun that has already been used earlier in the sentence. It can be used to join two sentences together. Examples: **who, whom, whose, which, that.**
Rhetorical question	A question that does not expect an answer.
Subject	Indicates *who* or *what* a sentence is about.
Subordinate clause	Depends on the main clause of a sentence for its meaning. Also called a *dependent clause.*
Superlative	The form of an *adjective* or *adverb* that is used to compare more than two nouns or verbs, e.g. **tallest, most useful, most slowly.**
Tense	The form of a *verb* that shows when an action takes place.
Present tense	Action happening now, e.g. **I eat,** or **I am eating.**
Past tense	Action that happened in the past, e.g. **She watched, She was watching, She has watched,** or **She had watched.**
Future tense	Action that is going to happen, e.g. **I shall/will see,** or **I am going to see.**
Verb	Expresses an *action* or indicates a *state of being.*
Auxiliary verb	Accompanies and helps a main verb, e.g. to form *tenses.*

YOUR NOTES